William Gilpin

Moral Contrasts

Or, the Power of Religion Exemplified Under Different Characters

William Gilpin

Moral Contrasts
Or, the Power of Religion Exemplified Under Different Characters

ISBN/EAN: 9783337025427

Printed in Europe, USA, Canada, Australia, Japan

Cover: Foto ©Thomas Meinert / pixelio.de

More available books at **www.hansebooks.com**

MORAL CONTRASTS:

OR,

THE POWER OF RELIGION

EXEMPLIFIED UNDER

DIFFERENT CHARACTERS.

BY WILLIAM GILPIN,

PREBENDARY OF SALISBURY, AND VICAR
OF BOLDRE, IN NEW FOREST.

LYMINGTON:

PRINTED BY J. B. RUTTER; AND SOLD BY
MESSRS. CADELL AND DAVIES, IN
THE STRAND, LONDON.

1798.

PREFACE.

SOME time ago I drew up a little contrast between a virtuous and a vicious character adapted to the lower people; and intended at first merely for the use of my own parish. It was afterwards printed for sale, at the desire of my bookseller;* and as it was better received than I imagined such a trifle could have been, I was induced to complete the plan by ano-

---

* Under the title of John Trueman and Richard Atkins, printed for R. Blamire, and now sold by Messrs. Cadell and Davies.

ther little work of the same kind, adapted to the higher ranks of people; to whom I now offer it.

To the two first characters, which are both *fictitious*, I have added two others, with a view to *improve the contrast*, and to throw a still stronger light on the power of religion. These two latter characters are taken from *real life*.

The former of them is extracted chiefly from a book entitled " Some " passages of the life, and death of " John, Earl of Rochester, written by " his own direction, on his death-bed, " by Gilbert Burnet, bishop of Salis-
" bury."

"bury."——The *whole* of the bishop's treatise, which records many things *not mentioned here*, is well worth the attentive perusal of every one, who would see in a strong light the ascendancy of religion over wickedness.—With the bishop's narrative is commonly printed a sermon preached at Lord Rochester's funeral, which contains many other remarkable particulars. I have extracted some of the most interesting from both.

The last of these little memoirs is the history of a *child of Nature*—a young African prince, of the name of Naimbanna, who was sent into England.

England by the Sierra Leone company, to be inſtructed in the chriſtian religion. The materials of this memoir conſiſt partly of extracts from the reports of that company—and partly of particulars received from thoſe, who kindly took on them the inſtruction of this young African.

An apology is perhaps due for thus mixing *fiction* and *reality* in the ſame work. But in *real* characters we cannot always procure the ſeveral circumſtances, and poſitions in life we wiſh to exhibit. And as to the impropriety of mixing them, in fact, I am inclined

clined to confider them all of the fame fpecies. The two firft of thefe memoirs do not mean to recommend themfelves under the idea of *fiction;* but as *pictures drawn from the life.* If indeed they had been embellifhed with romantic, or unnatural circumftances, they could not certainly have united with real life. In that cafe,

———Nec pes, nec caput uni
Reddatur formæ.———

But I fuppofe there is not a fingle incident in thefe fictions which hath not been exemplified at different times in a thoufand inftances in real life; tho perhaps they never all met toge-

together in any two perfons. They differ therefore, I conceive, from real life no otherwife, than as a landfcape compofed from felected parts of various countries differs from the portrait of fome real fcene. Both are equally copies from nature.—Nay perhaps the *fictitious* character is the more natural one. The deep repentance of Lord Rochefter, and the ingenuous mind of Naimbanna, which thefe pages prefent, are circumftances full as much, I fear, out of the common road of nature, as any, which occur in the two former of thefe memoirs.

MEMOIRS

OF

MR. WILLOUGHBY

AND

SIR JAMES LEIGH.

ERRATA.

PAGE

For *had turning* read *and turning* - - - - - 37
For *a room,* read *the room;* and for *those persons* read *these persons* - - - - - - - - 51
For *good-tempered man,* read *good tempered a man* - - - - - - - - - - - - - - - - - 75
For *no very short,* read *a very short* - - - - 101

A CATALOGUE of Mr. GILPIN's Works, fold by Meſſrs. CADELL and DAVIES, in the Strand.

An Expoſition of the New Teſtament, intended as an introduction to the ſtudy of the holy ſcriptures, by pointing out the leading ſenſe, and connection of the ſacred writers. Third Edition, 2 vols. 8vo.

Lectures on the Catechiſm of the Church of England Fourth Edition, 12mo.

Lives of ſeveral Reformers, of different Editions, and prices, the whole together 12s. 6d.

Eſſay on Prints. Fourth Edition, price 4s.

Pictureſque Remarks on the River Wye. Third Edition, 8vo. price 17s.

——————on the Lakes of Cumberland and Weſtmoreland, 2 vols. Third Edition, price 1l. 11s. 6d.

——————on the Highlands of Scotland, 2 vols. Second Edition, price 1l. 16s.

——————on Foreſt Scenery, 2 vols. Second Edition, price 1l. 16s.

Three Eſſays—on Pictureſque Beauty—on Pictureſque Travel—and on the art of ſketching Landſcape. Second Edition, price 10s. 6d.

Life of John Trueman and Richard Atkins, for the uſe of ſervant's-halls—farm-houſes—and cottages, price 10d. or 108 for 4l.

Account of William Baker, price 3d.

Mr. WILLOUGHBY was the son of a very worthy father, and of an excellent mother; both of whom took great pains in impressing his mind with an early sense of religion. As he grew up, his father resolved to educate him in a manner very different from the fashionable mode of educating youth. He was afraid of a public school. He was afraid also of a university either at home, or abroad: and still more he was

was afraid of foreign travel; which, in his opinion, afforded little advantage to an English gentleman.

He placed his son therefore at an early age under the care of a neighbouring clergyman who had no other charge; and of whose piety and learning he was well assured. With this worthy gentleman, young Mr. Willoughby passed several years with great advantage; making at different times, as his education advanced, excursions for amusement, into different parts of the kingdom, sometimes with his father, and sometimes with his tutor.

Mr. Willoughby in the mean time, was often taxed with bringing up his son in so recluse a manner. His reply was; he did not think our public schools, and universities, made religion so much the grand point of education, as he could wish. They made human learning he thought, take the lead too much. Besides, the dissipation of youth in this licentious age made him dread a connection with them. In soberer times he should have been less afraid. " I chuse ra-
" ther, said he, to pursue my own
" method. My first business is to
" make my son a good christian,
" which

"which is the foundation of every "thing that is useful, and beneficial. "I shall then endeavour to qualify "him for that station, in which Pro- "vidence hath placed him."

Accordingly, when he was about the age of eighteen, the old gentleman brought him home; and carrying him one day into his study, he seated him near his own elbow-chair; and taking him by the hand, "My dear Frank, "said he, I am now growing into years, "and wish to disincumber myself from "the management of my affairs. You "are now of an age to assist me: and "there is no assistance, which a fa-
"ther

" ther can have, so desirable as that
" of a well disposed son. Their inte-
" rests are the same. Besides, added
" he, as you are to be bred to your fa-
" ther's profession—that of a country
" gentleman—while you serve me,
" you will also be learning, if I may
" so speak, your own trade."

Nothing could be more agreeable to young Mr. Willoughby, than the idea of being of use to his father. He only feared his own inability. With the assistance however of an old steward, he hoped every thing would go on well. With him therefore at his elbow, he settled accounts—renewed

newed leafes—and eafed his father of all trouble, except that of now and then figning his name. And yet he had fufficient time for his books, and the indulgence of his tafte in the polite arts, of which he was extremely fond, and in which his father greatly encouraged him as a rational amufement.

One thing, in which his father employed him, was to pay regularly all his little penfions to poor widows, fuperannuated labourers, and old fervants, of whom he had feveral on his lift.

Among his own labourers, and thofe

those of his tenants, it was his custom also, when the parents were deserving people, to allow four guineas a year for every child above three. But when the eldest went out, the fourth was considered as a third. In paying all these little pensions, which were scattered about the country, Mr. Willoughby found no inconvenience, as he made them consistent with his usual exercise on horseback. It was an employment too, in which he found much pleasure, as he was every where joyfully received on so kind an errand; and found his own happiness more and more increased, the more he he became the instrument of happiness to others.

In the mean time his father carried him always with him to the sessions—the assizes—and county-meetings, to initiate him by degrees into the knowledge of such affairs, as might afterwards engage him. Thus by training him up in the business of a country gentleman, and the various offices of a useful life, he thought he had done more for him, than if he had sent him to the best university in Europe. When they came home from any public meeting, the old gentleman always assisted his son in making observations

servations on men, and things. If he had observed any gentleman, who had behaved with propriety, and was listened to with attention—or any, who had been loud, overbearing, and treated with neglect, he would remark to his son the propriety, or the impropriety of every thing he had seen.

While Mr. Willoughby was thus training up an affectionate son in the useful offices of life; and was about to give him more consequence by settling an independence upon him, he was suddenly carried off by a fit
of

of apoplexy, before his son had yet attained his twenty-second year.

In the neighbourhood of Mr. Willoughby lived Sir Thomas Leigh, whose eldest son was nearly about the age of Mr. Willoughby. Sir Thomas was one of those prudent parents, who blamed exceedingly the recluse manner, in which his neighbour Mr. Willoughby brought up his son; and gave a very different education to his own. He thought a knowledge of the world at large was indispensably necessary to a gentleman of fortune. To see the tricks, and obliquity of

man-

mankind with his own eyes, was the only way, he said, by which a young man could be taught to guard against them. Sir Thomas was what the world called a decent man. He was seldom guilty of any open breach of duty; but he had no great solicitude about religion; and thought accomplishments stood higher in the scale of life, than christian virtues. Under the impression of these ideas he sent his son to a public school, with plenty of money in his pocket to teach him the early use of it. And by the time the young man had gained a very fashionable knowledge in the art of spending

spending it, in which few made a greater proficiency, he was sent to the university, where he found himself in a more enlarged field for displaying his abilities. Here he soon became so well versed in every polite mode of expence, that his father's pocket, tho it had never been a close one to him, began seriously to complain. Sir Thomas apprehending therefore, what indeed he might have apprehended without much sagacity, that Jemmy had gotten into bad company, resolved prudently to break his connections, before it was too late. He hurried him away therefore immediately

mediately with a genteel young man, who attended him as a sort of something between a tutor and companion, to a foreign university.

It soon however appeared, that bad company may be found abroad, as well as at home, and that young Mr. Leigh had always the addrefs to get acquainted with the worſt.

But the moſt confummate effort of his genius, was, to corrupt his tutor; which was a matter of great importance to him: for while he himſelf was inceſſant in drawing bills, his truſty friend was equally aſſiduous in forming plauſible excuſes. Sometimes finding

finding gentle fault—sometimes palliating—and sometimes hinting at the young gentleman's better resolutions, he managed with such dexterity, that he kept himself free from all suspicion; and by that means was effectually enabled to assist his young friend in completely duping his father.

Sir Thomas however had now found by his banker's accounts, that he had gotten wrong a second time in his ideas of education. He called to mind therefore the old proverb, of *a rolling stone which gathers no moss*, and determined, that Jemmy should never reside long at any one place; but should

should travel from country to country; and so get an enlarged insight into the manners of men.

With this view he dispatched a trusty old Swiss servant to accompany him in his travels, with his pocket-book stuffed with recommendatory letters to all the English ministers at the several courts of Europe.

In consequence of these orders the two friends, who were then at Rouen, set out immediately for Paris. From thence they hurried away to Lyons. Turin received them next. There crossing the Alps, they found themselves in Italy, which they traversed

from

from the Po to the bay of Naples. During all thefe journeys, they inveftigated the manners of different countries in hotels—brothels—gaming-houfes, and theatres.—At Naples their career was ftopped. Mr. Leigh there received an account of his father's death; which was a joyful note to him, not only as he fucceeded to his title and eftate; but as nobody now could call him to account.

Thus thefe two young gentlemen, Mr. Willoughby, and Sir James Leigh inherited their paternal eftates nearly at the fame time. Mr. Willoughby

loughby could spend an income, clear of all incumbrances, of five thousand a year. Sir James Leigh's estate, independent of his mother's settlement, brought him in more than double that sum. The two young gentlemen had been acquainted from their infancy; and now lived within half a dozen miles of each other; but being men of very different dispositions and pursuits, their intimacy, which had never been great, dwindled into a few ceremonious visits.

Their different dispositions began soon to appear. Mr. Willoughby fol-

following the fteps of a judicious father, was in no hafte to make any alteration in his houfe, grounds, or manner of living. What fchemes of improvement he had, he prudently confidered, before he put them in execution. He thought it prudent alfo to lay by a little money for thefe purpofes, left they might involve him in difficulties, from which he could not eafily free himfelf.

In the mean time, none of his father's penfions, or charities, which were very confiderable, were difcontinued. But he paid nothing with fo much pleafure as a hundred a year,

which

which his father had settled for life upon his old tutor. He would gladly have doubled it; but the old gentleman would not suffer him. "Be con"tent, said he, my dear Franky, (which was his common mode of accosting him) "be content with what your "father has done. He was a very "generous man; and if you go be"yond *him*, I fear you will exceed."

While Mr. Willoughby acted this prudent part, his neighbour, Sir James, set off in full career. He had scarce taken possession of his estate, when he had half the workmen of the country about him on different projects. But his favorite scheme was a superb pile of stabling, which he built at a vast expence; and then furnished it with a great variety of the best horses, for the road—the field—the race—and the carriage. By the time his stables were completely filled, he had not only consumed all the ready money his father had left him, which was no inconsiderable sum; but was obliged to make up deficiencies by borrowing seven thousand pounds. The yearly expence of this vast establishment of grooms, and horses, to which he added a kennel

nel of hounds, was not so little as eighteen hundred pounds.

In the mean time, as he detested all thoughts of marriage, he seduced from her friends, a beautiful young woman, the sister of a lieutenant of a man of war, whose dependent state as a mistress would free him, he hoped, from all the inconveniences, which he dreaded in a wife. But he had made a few small mistakes, as most people do, who amuse themselves with these licentious calculations. In fact, he knew nothing of her, beyond her personal charms; nor had made any observations on her manners and behaviour. Under a meek and modeſt demeanor ſhe concealed a very violent temper; and under an apparent ſimplicity of manners, which indicated a ductile ſpirit, ſhe poſſeſſed a very obſtinate and refractory one. Her inſolence ſoon began to appear; and was ſuch, that he was daily more or leſs diſconcerted by it. From the firſt, it was her object to make herſelf the entire miſtreſs of his family: and from leſs proceeding to more, ſhe ordered coaches, and horſes, when ſhe pleaſed—ſhe directed his motions to different places—ſhe turned away his ſervants

—and,

—and even sometimes affronted his company. She had the art however, when she saw she had carried matters too far, to throw in a little soothing submission: and as he was fascinated with her charms, his wrath, tho daily raised, was as often assuaged. Every action of her life shewed she despised him: but she knew her power; and tho she delighted in teizing, and making him miserable, she still held him in the bonds of inchantment.

Mr. Willoughby's ideas of domestic happiness were very different.
He

He thought a marriage founded in virtue, mutual affection, and mutual interest, gave him a better chance for happiness, than the loose indulgence of a dissolute passion.

About a mile from his house stood a good old mansion, which had often been used as a jointure-house by the widows of the family. Here Mr. Willoughby's mother chose rather to reside, with an only daughter, than to live with her son. The company he was unavoidably obliged to keep, she thought might be some little intrusion on the quiet of her morning and evening hours, which she generally spent alone

alone in her chamber, over her bible. But tho the families lived separately, the distance was so small, that they were generally together.

Miss Willoughby had an intimate friend, a young lady of her own age, of the name of Henneage, who generally spent a part of every summer with her. Here Mr. Willoughby, of course, frequently saw her, and as often admired her. But his behaviour was so very distant, that it was impossible she could take the least notice of it. At length, when he was fully assured of her good qualities, and his own resolution, he ventured to open

his

his mind to his mother, and sister. He soon found he could do nothing more agreeable to them, than to pay his addresses to Miss Henneage. His sister indeed told him, she always suspected he had an affection for her; "Not, said she, from any thing I "ever observed in your behaviour; "but because I thought it was im- "possible you could look with indif- "ference on such excellence."

Matters being in this train, Mr. Willoughby left it to his mother to open the affair to Miss Henneage; which she did one evening as the young lady came into her chamber to
ask

aſk, if ſhe had any objection to her taking a walk with Nancy to the dairy-farm? " I have no objection at all, my dear Lucy, ſaid Mrs. Willoughby; and now you muſt tell me, whether you have any objection to what I am going to aſk *you*." On mentioning the affair, Mr. Willoughby's pleaſing form, and manly addreſs, and virtues, that were the theme of every tongue, came ſuddenly riſing at once to her imagination: a ſort of palpitating confuſion overſpead her whole frame; and ſhe could anſwer only with a bluſh. She was above any coquetiſh airs: and the old lady

lady needed no other language to convince her, she had seen her son with as favourable eyes, as he had seen her. " Well, my dear, said Mrs. Wil-
" loughby, go, and take your walk
" with your friend; only don't stay
" out so late, as you did last wed-
" nesday."

Among other things, which passed between the two friends, in their evening walk, on this important occasion, Miss Henneage said, it had been her secret intention, as she was so well provided for by her father, to lead a single life, and spend her time, and fortune, like her good aunt, in being of
service

service to her neighbours. " And I "believe said she, nothing but such a "temptation as your brother has "thrown in my way, could have "altered my intention."

Matters being now settled, and Mr. Willoughby pressing for an early day, she said, as she was not yet nineteen, she could not think of changing her state of life, till at least two years more had passed over her. To this Mr. Willoughby reluctantly consented, upon condition she would spend that time with his mother, and sister. Miss Henneage laughed, and said, she did not ask his consent, nor thought herself

herself tyed by any of his conditions. She was yet her own mistress; and intended to spend the next two years with her good aunt, as she had always done.

As her aunt lived at the distance of thirty miles, this interdict was a severe trial to Mr. Willoughby. But he was obliged to submit; and had only the satisfaction of calling her a cruel, hard-hearted girl. She had the pleasure however to find, that her judicious young friend intirely approved her resolution.

But tho the two years went heavily on, Mr. Willoughby had the happiness

ness at length to find, they had an end. *His* happiness was the happiness of the country. When he brought his lady home from her aunt's, the whole neighbourhood was in a tumult of joy. Among other compliments paid him on the occasion, a very elegant copy of verses was laid, by an unknown hand, upon his hall-table, intitled *Francis and Lucy, or the happy marriage.*

In the mean time, Sir James Leigh was carrying on his *improvements*, as he called them, with a profusion of expence, that astonished every body.

If

If you walked near his house, you saw groups of labourers, here, and there, and every where—removing ground—widening rivers—building bridges—or employed in other expensive operations; none of which had been well considered, or was conducted with the least taste, or judgment; for he had too high an opinion of himself to follow the advice of any one. His projects were all in opposition to nature. He seemed to delight in difficulties. If a piece of rising ground stood in his way, instead of casting about, how to turn it into a beauty, he would immediately order it, tho of conder-
able

able dimenfions, to be removed. Such violence is generally efteemed by all judicious improvers, as abfurd, as it is expenfive.

Within doors he had a large family of ill-governed fervants; who being haughtily treated, and ill-paid, had no regard for their mafter; and made no fcruple of paying themfelves by every little fraudulent exaction; and by purloining whatever they could lay their hands upon. Every thing without doors was in the fame ftile of profufion. The wafte and pilfering in his ftables, and other out-houfes, was enormous.

Money however now, as it may well be supposed, began to grow scarce. Borrowing was his first resource. But as he had different modes of spending money, it became necessary to have different modes of procuring it. As one of the easiest, a friend suggested to him the method of borrowing money on annuities; and introduced him to a grave gentleman, who had always money ready to assist unfortunate young men. From this friend of his necessity he could obtain, whenever the hour of distress came upon him, three, or four thousand pounds with no more trouble than

that

that of figning his name. Poor Sir James, who never looked beyond the preffing exigence, had neither the arithmetic, nor the forefight to calculate how much his eftate diminifhed, as his wants were relieved. The courfe of things however ran on, notwithftanding his fupinenefs; and at the end of ten years, he found he could not fpend annually, out of his large eftate above four thoufand pounds. All this however did not open his eyes. He ftill went blindly on.

His prudent neighbour, in the mean time, had carryed on his improveprovements in a different manner. He went on flowly; but at the end of feven years much was to be feen. His father had never fhewn any inftances of tafte; nor had he ever pretended to it. The fon had more refined ideas; but indulged them with great propriety. He not only kept within his abilities; but by collecting labourers at thofe times, when other work was not eafily to be had, he made his improvements anfwer the double end of advantage to himfelf; and of convenience to his neighbours.

Then again by laying out his plans judicioufly at firft, he had never occa-

fion

sion to alter them afterwards— Many people spend as much in altering, and undoing, as in their original work; which was poor Sir James's case.—He had three times altered the course of a rivulet, that ran through his park; and had as often changed the situation of a bridge. And what was singular, his second thought was generally worse than the first; and his third, than the second. The bare alterations, had turning the front, of a *Temple of Fame*, cost him nearly five hundred pounds. The country people gave it afterwards the name of the *Temple of Folly*.— Mr. Willoughby's improvements were chargeable with none of these ill-digested absurdities. What he did, was done.

It was one of his great rules also, never to fight with nature. Her clue guided all his operations. Where she led, he followed: and thus, at the same time he formed the most beautiful scenes, and saved more than three fourths of the expence, which his precipitate neighbour would have incurred by attempting the same thing. Every autumn he made a little addition to his plan; but he meant the full completion of his design to be the amusement of his life. He judiciously

ously considered, that when a plan is finished, it often becomes insipid: but a growing work seldom fails to be a constant source of pleasure.

That great error of suffering any single part to swallow up the rest, he avoided. Sir James Leigh had confessedly the grandest stables in the country; but they were the stables of a prince, not of a country gentleman: they were far beyond the scale of his house, or any of its appendages. In Mr. Willoughby's improvements, and whole economy, you saw nothing but propriety, and proportion. No gentleman made a more elegant ap-
pear-

pearance—rode a better horse—or had a more genteel equipage. If you entered his house, you saw every thing in the same stile of elegance, and economy: and if you looked into his stables, you saw a sufficient number of good, useful horses; but no superfluous expence. You saw neither race-horse, nor hunter. Racing he considered as gambling: and as to hunting, he thought its many disagreeable accompaniments took away from it every idea of an amusement.

As to his servants, many of them were a kind of heir-looms. They had lived with his father—had known
him

him from a boy—and were attached to his intereſt: while every new ſervant readily adopted the ways of ſo orderly a ſociety. Indeed his ſervants were generally the children of his tenants, and labourers, whom he took early into his houſe; and advanced as they deſerved. From this way of making up his family, he ſaid, he found great advantage. He had not only his own eye upon his ſervants; but the eye alſo of their parents. In the mean time, his ſervice, which was indeed an *inheritance*, was always anxiouſly ſought after. Such of his ſervants who had lived long with him—

him—had behaved well, as they generally did—and were desirous of settling in the world, he always provided for; procuring for one a place, and giving another a farm. For their reception he had several little tenements scattered about his estate—some of them within the precincts of his park, which he used to call his outposts. "It would be a difficult thing, he would say, for a trespasser to attack me on any side with so many faithful eyes about me."

Many of these tenements were in sight of his house—his garden, or his park: and they were built and contrived

trived in such a manner, as to adorn several little scenes within his view. Some of his neighbours thought these tenements would have had a better effect, if they had been built in the form of churches and abbeys, and castles. But Mr. Willoughby's taste was more simple. He had a great dislike to affectation in every shape; and thought the plain ornaments of nature the most pleasing decorations of a cottage. A tufted grove—a winding road—the margin of a lake—the banks of a river, or some other natural circumstance, were much more
pleasing

pleasing to him, than those pompous trifles, which many people admire.

Among servants brought up, and considered in the affectionate manner, in which Mr. Willoughby considered his servants, there was nothing of that riot, waste, and profusion, which were endless among the servants at the other house. A careful, old housekeeper, a butler, and a groom, who had long managed his kitchen, his cellar, and his stables, saw to the end of every thing. Thus altho Mr. Willoughby lived as hospitably, as generously, and as respectably as any gentleman in the country, and had made

made many improvements around him—yet by cutting off all needlefs expence, and by introducing ftrict economy into fuch expences, as he thought needful, he not only lived within his income; but he had laid by two, or three thoufand pounds, as a little fund againft emergencies; to which every year he added fomething. And if any one mentioned to him his acts of bounty, or generofity, he would fay, " Do not tell me of thefe things. I get fcandaloufly rich, whatever you may fuppofe." Indeed he ufed always to affert that what he gave,

made

made him richer, in a literal senſe, inſtead of poorer.

The great difference between Sir James Leigh's ideas of expence, and Mr. Willoughby's, was this. Sir James denied himſelf in nothing. Whatever fooliſh ſcheme came into his head, let the price be what it might, he confidered only the immediate gratification.—Mr. Willoughby, on the other hand. denyed himſelf many things, not becauſe he ſhould not have taken pleaſure in them, but becauſe he thought them inadequate to the price he was to pay: that is, in ſhort, he confidered himſelf as the
ſteward

steward of heaven's bounty; and thought he should have acted as unjustly towards his great master, if he had lavished that bounty improperly, as his own steward would have done, if he had embezzled his rents. *Give an account of thy stewardship*, was a regulating principle with him in all his expences.

If in any amusement Mr. Willoughby exceeded, it was in the purchase of pictures: and yet in this, he acted with great judgment. If a collector resolve to purchase such pictures only as are curious, and capital, he may be led into any expence. But

pictures

pictures of this kind are often less prized for their excellence, than for the master's name, or some other circumstance; which has little connection with their real value. Much better pictures may be frequently bought at a lower price, tho the connoiseur hath not set his stamp upon them. Among pictures of this second class Mr. Willoughby made his collection. He had a good eye; and furnished his whole house for a sum of money, which the curious collector sometimes gives for a single piece. And yet he was not quite satisfied with his expences on this head; tho it was the only

only expensive amusement, in which he indulged himself. "I have been looking (said he, one day to a friend) into my picture-accounts; and I find the pictures in this house have cost me the shameful sum of one thousand, five hundred, and thirty-two pounds. But my father, good man, used to encourage me in these expences; and perhaps his encouragement may have carried me too far."——This self-conviction did not arise in any degree from his incurring an expence that was inconvenient to him; but merely from the fear of having spent on an amusement what might have been spent on a more proper occasion.

Several of his apartments had been adorned in his father's time, with family-pictures. But they were such miserable representatives of some very respectable people, that Mr. Willoughby used to say, when he looked at them, they belied every anecdote he had ever heard in their favour.

He did not however send his family-pictures, as many do, into a garret; but hung them up in a large room, which he dedicated to the *Manes of his Ancestors.* This room he contrived to make one of the most interesting apartments of his houſe. Tho the pictures were bad, the frames were rich; and made a ſplendid appearance. Each portrait was numbered; and theſe numbers referred to a book, which lay on a table covered with green cloth, in the middle of a room. In this book he gave a modeſt account of all the perſons, men, and women, who were aſſembled on the walls; which accounts he prefaced by ſaying, that " as many of thoſe perſons had " deſerved better treatment, than they " had found from the hands of the " artiſts, who had pourtrayed them, " he had endeavoured with filial piety "to his anceſtors, to make up the deficiency."——The following inſtance will ſhew the manner in which he drew up theſe ſhort accounts.

No. IX.

"This gentleman, who from the whimſical manner, in which the painter has ſurrounded him with birds, might be taken for a bird-catcher, is Mr. Willoughby, the ornithologiſt, ſon of Sir Francis Willoughby, (No. VIII.) who hath juſt been mentioned. At the age of thirty ſeven, at which he died, he had attained more learning, and know-

" knowledge in various branches,
" especially in natural history, than
" almost any man of his time. And
" what is still more, he hath ever been
" looked up to by his grateful poste-
" rity, as a pattern of virtue.—See
" his works in the library, (S. 15. 7.)
" and an account of him by his friend
" Mr. Ray, the celebrated naturalist,
" who revised, and published them.
" Mr. Ray in his preface to his Orni-
" thology, says, *What rendered Mr.*
" *Willoughby most commendable, was*
" *his eminent virtue, and goodness. I*
" *cannot say, that I ever observed such*
" *a confluence of excellent qualities in*
" one

" *one person.* Mr. Ray then enume-
" rates the several *excellent qualities,*
" which he had observed in him.

Thus Mr. Willoughby had the ingenuity to turn a number of bad pictures into a set of very entertaining companions. For as the persons they represented, had figured in various professions of life, and many of them very reputably, he had collected from tradition, letters, and family-records, many amusing anecdotes of most of them.

With three of these pictures he was a little perplexed. Two of them were by Vandyck, and the third by Sir

Peter

Peter Lely: and as all the three were good, he would have been glad to have hung them up in one of his best rooms. But on confideration, he hung all together, and graced the bad with the good.

Of tafte, in any fhape, except the moft grofs and fenfual, Sir James Leigh had no idea. Of books he knew nothing. He was totally illiterate; and in every branch of fcience intirely ignorant. On his intimacy with the polite arts indeed he valued himfelf greatly: but his knowledge of them went no further, than that kind of
infipid

insipid, insignificant prattle, which distinguishes a coxcomb. Few people therefore who had the least pretension, either to taste, or reading, or virtue, or any thing commendable, ever came near him. The company that frequented his house, were the spendthrifts—the horse-racers—the gamesters, and other profligate young fellows of the country. Their table-conversation was commonly made up of the occurrences of the last horse-race—the last cock-fight—or the last hunting-match—perhaps at what tavern such a dish was best dressed—or where the best wine of such a kind

was

was fold. The brothel too was a common theme among them. And all this converfation was larded with oaths—prophanenefs—and obfcenity. Loud debates too on thefe important fubjects would often enfue—many clamouring at once—while others were finging filthy fongs and catches—till, as the hour grew late, and bottle after bottle, had been called for—all this horrid din funk by degrees into the beaftly ftupidity of intoxication.

All fuch intemperance and irregularity, tho not immediately felt in a young conftitution, yet will fap it by degrees: and Sir James found, before he he was forty, that his vicious pleasures, and common modes of life, had even then begun to call him to a severe account.

In the mean time all those disgusting scenes, which were acted in the parlour, were acted over again in the servant's hall; where they were heightened, if possible, with still more abominable brutality.

To all this, Mr. Willoughby's family was a direct contrast. He was rather a retired man himself, and not fond of company. But his station in life brought many people about him; tho.

tho he mixed freely with thofe only, who were men of approved character. With thefe he was always on the beft terms. The clergyman of the parifh, who was a religious and fenfible man, and about his own age, was much his companion. Befides him, there were a few more men of letters in the country; with whofe elegant and inftructive converfation he always mixed with great pleafure. But when the difcourfe did not turn on literary fubjects, nothing was ever heard at his table, that was not at leaft innocent, chearful, and good-humoured. Often it turned on modes

of

of easing the distresses of the poor, and of adding to their comforts. Most of the benevolent schemes, carried on in the parish, of which there were many, took their rise at Mr. Willoughby's table.

At such a board, it may easily be imagined, no irregularity could be admitted. Mr. Willoughby himself lived with that temperance, and sobriety, which all wise men would practise even on worldly motives, tho they did not consider those virtues in the light of christian duties. And in his company no man, if he were even inclined, durst exceed. Saints are

com-

commonly painted with a glory round their heads. A sort of splendid atmosphere somewhat of this kind surrounds good men, within the influence of which nothing indecent dare approach.

The amusements of the family were as rational as their conversation. Mr Willoughby's library was a room for use, not for shew. It was adorned with globes, maps, and other suitable appendages. He spent much of his time among his books. Cards were never seen in his house; an aversion to which he inherited from his father, who always thought them the most insipid

sipid of all amusements. A game at chess he would sometimes play with the vicar; which was commonly a sharp contention between them; and often drew on more eagerness, than Mr. Willoughby liked; each having the vanity to think he was the better player.

In summer also bowls were much in fashion; in which Mr. Willoughby was superior to all his antagonists. The gentlemen who commonly frequented his green, used to laugh, and say, they would vote him out of all their matches; for they were sure he exercised himself with his bowls alone.
—And

—And this indeed was true enough: for it was his ufual practice, when he found himfelf languid at his book, to ftep out at a back-door in his ftudy, which opened near the bowling-green, and refresh himfelf there with a little exercife.

But his amufements of every kind were moderate, and rational; and his fervants having no examples before them, but what tended to their improvement, fell naturally into all thofe modes of quietnefs, regularity and civility, which appeared fo amiable in their mafter; whofe endeavour they plainly faw, was to make them happy,

and

and gratify them in every thing that was proper for them.

The employment, and amusements of the neighbouring family were very different. Sir James Leigh acted like a man, who thought a large fortune had been given him merely to spend in different modes of dissipation. Gaming was his predominant passion. Nothing ingrossed his thoughts so much: nor was any one welcome at his house, who was not addicted to cards, and dice.

Cards, and dice likewise descended into the servant's-hall, where the spirit

of

of gaming, only in a lower ſtile, reigned with all its aſſociate paſſions, as much as in the parlour.

But his gaming in the country was comparatively mere *amuſement*. In town, it was a *buſineſs*. At home he played generally with his equals; and tho the practice was vile, it was ſeldom ruinous. But when he went to London, and became a *cully* (as all young adventurers are) in the hands of *profeſſed maſters* in the art of gaming, it was dreadful indeed. And tho it would be as difficult to perſuade theſe *profeſſors* to relinquiſh an art by which they live, as it would be to per-

persuade their brethren of the road to lay aside their crape and pistols; yet one should suppose so many fatal examples might have some weight with the poor *cullies*, who are drawn into their snares. They should recollect the cautious answer once given to another plunderer;

———————— *Nos vestigia terrent*
Omnia te adversum spectantia, nulla retrorsum.

Poor Sir James was a *cully* of the first order. His servants used to give out, they had rare doings at their house in London. Their master was generally all day in bed: and their
mistress

mistress was seldom at home. Indeed Sir James commonly spent his nights in a gaming-house; and retired to bed about sunrise.

The same happiness which reigned among Mr. Willoughby's *servants*, was diffused among his *tenants*. With them he lived upon the easiest terms. When an old tenant renewed his lease, his rent was never raised, unless some improvement in the land made the reason evident, and the tenant himself saw the propriety of it. It was Mr. Willoughby's great pleasure to see all his tenants thrive under him; and to be of service to such, as had large families, by assisting the parents in providing for them. In cases of unavoidable misfortunes, he would often forgive rents: and in cases of less urgency he had provided a fund, from which he lent small sums without interest, either to repair some little loss—or to purchase with advantage at a good market.—When a tenant, or a labourer died, he had especial regard to the widow, and family, which he considered as a trust devolved upon himself, if their circumstances required it. If the widow chose to keep the farm, his steward, or himself, was always

ways ready to give his advice, or aſſiſtance.—Beſides theſe open inſtances of kindneſs, he was continually doing acts of unknown generoſity: and in ſhort was conſidered, wherever his connections extended, as a kind of centre, which drew to it the difficulties, and diſtreſſes of the whole neighbourhood around him.

One indulgence he gave his tenants, which was of no ſolid advantage indeed, but very gratifying. He allowed them all to kill game upon their own farms—but he allowed this liberty only to the tenant himſelf, not to his ſervants. And he uſed to ſay, he he believed he was a gainer by it: for the tenant thus interested, kept off poachers, and was careful to preserve the game. Whereas, among Sir James's tenants, it was not an uncommon thing, when any of them found a nest of eggs in their fields, to crush them. " We have no advantage, " they would say, from the birds our-" selves, why should we feed them for " others—especially for such a land-" lord as ours?" In the mean time, Mr. Willoughby's table was plentifully supplied. One or other of the tenants was continually sending him in the season, a hare, or a pheasant,

or

or a couple of partridges: and when he wanted game, on any emergence, his gamekeeper could eafily get intelligence where to find it.

It was his great pleafure, when he rode out, to call on one, or other of his tenants; to whom he had always fomething to fay, that was pleafing; or fomething to propofe that was ufeful. In fhort, he confidered them as a part of his family; and was beloved and popular among them, beyond what can be imagined.

Very different was the intercourfe between Sir James Leigh and his tenants

ants. Nothing pleasing ever passed between them. The steward, and the attorney were the only agents. Rents were raised.—Instant payments were demanded.—Misfortunes were never considered.—Seizures were made.—Guns, and dogs were taken away—Every thing was managed with harshness. He never wished to conciliate people by acts of kindness; but to draw them to his purposes by acts of oppression.—An honest farmer, who lived in my neighbourhood, gave me the following relation.

"A few years ago, said he, I rented a little farm under Sir James Leigh.

He

He was then very busy with his hounds: tho I believe now, poor man! that matter, as well as others, are pretty well over with him. However he then kept two packs of different kinds; and used to put out the young hounds among his farmers, and tenants. Two of his fox-hounds were appointed for me. But as I had young children, and did not much like such company among them, I sent them back to his huntsman with a civil excuse. I was told I should suffer for it: and indeed I did. He let his fences go down in some grounds, which bordered on a large meadow

meadow of mine—the only one, which I intended for hay. I complained over and over, that his cattle were continually trespassing in my meadow: but I could get no redress. I am sure he let his fences go down on purpose: and I lost more than ten pounds that year by the mischief, that was done me. After this, I believe, nobody durst refuse his hounds.——He served another of his tenants, John Ellis, continued the farmer, the same kind of ill-natured trick. What Ellis had done to disoblige him, I forget: but I am sure it must have been some trifling thing, for

for Ellis was as good tempered man as any in England. Whatever it was however Sir James took high offence, and shewed his revenge by locking up a gate (over which unhappily the leafe had left him a power) that led to the farmer's yard. By this piece of tyranny he obliged poor Ellis to carry his loaden waggons a mile and a half about."

Thus, in short, the landlord and tenants were always in such a state of war, and disagreeable fermentation, that while Mr. Willoughby's farms were all well let; and half a dozen candidates appeared for every one that was

was vacant, Sir James had the mortification to hear, that several of his best farms were untenanted. They were of course managed by his steward and attorney, who being ill-paid, took good care to pay themselves; so that after the farms had passed through their hands, they produced little or nothing to the landlord. The only solace he had, on these occasions, was to curse his people all round; and swear he was beset on all hands by a pack of rogues, and rascals; and that he did not believe there was a grain of honesty on the face of the earth.

The

The intercourse also of these two gentlemen with their tradesmen, was as different as every other part of their conduct. Nothing could be more unpunctual than Sir James Leigh. He never sent for a bill; and when it was sent to him, no notice was taken of it. When the tradesman complained, he was told, the bill had been mislaid; and was ordered to send another—or he was told, that several articles were charged in so extraordinary a manner, that it would take some time to look them over. The truth was, no money could be found—especially for such pur-

purposes.—Sometimes indeed, when he had had a run of ill-luck at play, he was put to all his shifts even to procure a few guineas. In the mean time, some of his tradesmen would hasten payment by attorney's letters; and others would refuse to serve him longer.

All this gave him little distress. He had no regard for any thing, in which honour, or honesty, or even bare decency was concerned. He had as little for his own interest, which suffered at all points by thus putting himself intirely into the hands of others, and disabling himself from either

either rectifying a mistake, or guarding against a fraud. In short, if he could dexterously evade the pressing moment, it was all he desired.

In the mean time, Mr. Willoughby's affairs were managed with the utmost regularity. He knew the contents of each bill, and could easily check an improper charge.—Very exact people are often solicitous to pay all their bills at the end of every week, or some other short period. But such rigid punctuality is sometimes inconvenient to tradesmen; who rather wish, when their money
is

is fafe, to let it lie, till they have occafion to ufe it. Of this Mr. Willoughby was aware: and wifhing always to accomodate himfelf as much as poffible, to the convenience of others, he defired all his tradefmen to fend in their accounts, when it was moft agreeable to themfelves. They fhould be anfwered immediately. Only for his own convenience he defired, that none of them might ftand out longer than half a year.

But the moft effential difference between thefe two gentlemen, was in the article of religion. In Mr. Willoughby's loughby's family you immediately saw you were in a chriftian country. That beautiful fimplicity, and decorum of manners, which may be called the garb of religion, might be feen in every part of it: and the more you were converfant in it, the more you faw of its religious deportment. Every morning and evening, the bell rang for prayers.. Whether company was in the houfe, or not, it made no difference. Ceremony to man was never fuffered to interfere with a duty to God. Religious books were often read. Bibles, and other good books were feen lying on parlour-windows, and tables; and it was thought no impropriety to converse on religious subjects. Sunday was strictly observed. Mr. Willoughby and his family, with as many of the servants, as could be spared, went regularly to church—the sacrament was frequented—and great care was taken to keep up a religious impression among the servants. Sunday was never a day of invitation, and company. The servants therefore had as much respite as possible from the business of the parlour, the kitchen, and the stable.

As

As to christianity, in Sir James Leigh's family, it was out of the question. There was not even the least sign of religious decorum. You could not distinguish Sunday from any other day. Cards, and gaming, and drinking, were indiscriminately practised. The servants followed the example of their master; and if any of them was better disposed, and shewed the least degree of seriousness, he was immediately laughed out of it. Sir James's house indeed lay under so bad a name, that no young persons, either men, or women, who had any regard for their characters, would live there:

there: so that in fact, it was filled with such servants only, as nobody else would hire: nor indeed would any decent person hire a servant that had lived in so disreputable a family.

While Mr. Willoughby led the respectable life we have seen in his own neighbourhood, and was beloved, wherever he was known, an event came on, which shewed, he was equally respected throughout the county. At the general election a candidate offered himself, by no means acceptable to the general sense of the freeholders. But as nobody opposed him, he must of of courfe be elected. In this dilemma the gentlemen of the county, threw their eyes on Mr Willoughby, as a popular man—of good fortune—of an eftablished character—of an ancient family, long feated in the county, and every way the moft likely to draw the efteem of all parties. Mr. Willoughby told them he was not ambitious of ferving in parliament; but at all times attentive to the interefts of the county. As he thought it imprudent however to rifk his fortune in a contefted election, he hoped they would excufe his ftipulating for fupport. On this head he was made perfectly eafy;

easy; but at the same time assured, that if he would only declare himself, all opposition would cease. This assurance was well founded. It was no sooner known, that Mr. Willoughby offered himself, than the unanimous voice of the county appeared in his favour—the offensive candidate declined; and Mr. Willoughby was elected at the trifling expence of two hundred pounds— even which, the gentlemen of the county were desirous to pay, if he would have suffered them.

When he was in the house, he was respected by the minister, and often voted

voted with him: but he was not of his phalanx, and as often voted againſt him. From all favours he kept aloof; conſidering them as bribes, which were in ſome ſhape to be repaid. This diſintereſted conduct gave him ſo much credit in the houſe, that all the young members who had not addicted themſelves to party; but meant honeſtly to their country, thought they could not do better, than look up to Mr. Willoughby; and in all queſtions to follow his lead.

At the time when Mr. Willoughby was thus complimented by the gentlemen

tlemen of his county with a seat in parliament (which by the way they would never allow him afterwards to relinquish, till age made it a burden to him) Sir James Leigh in the neighbouring county, received as great an affront. He was exactly in the case of the offensive candidate, who had been antagonist to Mr. Willoughby, having obtruded himself against the inclination of all the leading gentlemen of the county, by whom he was thoroughly despised. A warm opposition was immediately set on foot. With his usual folly and disregard to consequences, he obstinately persevered;

severed; and was at length disgracefully thrown out, after he had spent, at the lowest calculation, twenty-five thousand pounds.—This was a heavy stroke upon his affairs, already greatly in the wane. He sought parliament indeed only as an asylum; or, if possible, to better his fortune: but by this unsuccessful attempt, he found his difficulties doubly increased. Some of his best tenements, and farms had already been disposed of, to silence his creditors, rather than to pay them. The best part of his estate was deeply mortgaged: and all his timber was cut down and sold.

Many

Many thousand trees were felled, which were still in a growing state. In short, his extravagancies of various kinds had run him quite aground; and this last election-affair had almost compleated his ruin.

Another disagreeable business also happened soon after the election. Sir James's mother had a settlement upon his estate of two thousand pounds a year, which had never been regularly paid. But at this time, the arrears were very large. Having made many ineffectual demands, she called upon him one morning; and after much heat and passion on both sides, she left

left him with a threat to put the affair into her lawyer's hands; which she did soon afterwards, and obliged him to pay in one sum near eleven thousand pounds, which he now found it very difficult to procure.

More than twenty years had now elapsed, since these two gentlemen had taken possession of their estates. During the first six, or seven years, we have seen Sir James carrying on such immense works, as astonished every body. But they had all long since been discontinued. One foolish project after another, had subsided. Nothing

thing was finished. The whole compass of his intended improvements was now a scene of wild, expensive desolation. What he had *done*, and what he had *undone*—what he had *begun*, and what he had yet only *planned*, were all blended together in one mass of confusion.

In the mean time Mr. Willoughby's improvements, which had gone on leisurely, had now attained great perfection. His trees were well-grown; and he had the satisfaction to see the plan, which he had originally formed with so much judgment, now opening

more

more and more into scenes of beauty. Every thing was in excellent order: his trees, and his shrubs were healthy: his lawns and his walks perfectly neat. It was easy to see, the hand, which had executed all this elegance, was still extended over it.

His farms too, and all the *profitable* parts of his estate, were in the same excellent order. While poor Sir James had not a farm house, that was not almost in ruins, Mr. Willoughby's estate was a model of regularity, and good management. It was one of his great pleasures to see his tenants under good roofs; and he thought nothing

was

was loft by making every thing convenient about them. What timber he cut down, was only such as called for the axe; and in its room he planted thousands of trees all over his domains, wherever wood could possibly grow with advantage—in the corners of fields particularly; which mode of planting, if it be managed properly, turns a field into a lawn.—By judicious persons it was calculated, that by planting, draining, and other improvements, he had increased the value of his estate, since he took possession of it, at least fifty thousand pounds. And tho he seldom raised his old tenants,

ants, yet in his new leafes, tho they were always moderate, he added several hundred pounds to his yearly rental.

The laſt event of Sir James's career was the moſt miſerable of all. The woman, with whom he lived, was now become intolerable to him. Indeed ſhe had been one cauſe, and no inconſiderable one, of the ruin of his affairs. Her debts, which he had twice paid, amounted to ſums of conſequence. Her very dreſs required the rental of a good farm to ſupport. Nothing was too expenſive for her.

In

In short, she was the very genius of prodigality. Her girls also, (for she had five) vyed in finery with the first-rate misses in the country: tho in the article of education, it must be allowed, an intire saving had been made.

While her youth, and beauty lasted, she knew how to assuage any tumult she might have raised; and long therefore continued to reign the intire mistress of his family. But five, and twenty years, joined to an irregular life, had now effaced her charms. Her elegant form was become heavy and bloated. Her fine complexion was grown red and pimpled. She had

had loft feveral of her teeth: and the natural violence of her temper, having chaced away all the rofy fmiles, and dimples of youth, had taken ftern poffeffion of all her features. As the means of foothing, therefore were gone, a continued fcene of quarrel, animofity, and bitternefs enfued. What was at firft only diflike on one fide, had now changed into a thorough difguft on both.

Sir James had long wifhed to rid himfelf of this incumbrance: but fhe had fuch an afcendancy over him, at firft by her beauty, and afterwards by the violence of her temper, that he
never

never could, indeed he never durst, propose it. Wearied at length however by her extravagance, and provoking insolence, he determined, at all events, to rouse himself, and throw off an evil, which was now beyond all sufferance. He told her therefore plainly, that he could keep her in his house no longer; and that she might repair to such a place (a house of his own in a distant village) where she should find he had not left her destitute.

No mad heroine on a stage, could display more fury, than she did on this occasion. " What! after se-
" ducing

"ducing her, and robbing her of her innocence, did he mean to turn her out of his houfe? Was fhe, and her poor girls to go begging about the country?—No: fhe vowed revenge. She did not fet her own life at a farthing in comparifon with her revenge: and if he dared to mention fuch an infult to her again, fhe would fhew him, what an injured, and inraged woman could do."

Soon afterwards, her brother, the lieutenant, appeared upon the ftage. He entered the houfe rudely; and without any ceremony, told Sir James

James in a surly tone, that he should find his poor injured sister had a friend, who would revenge her wrongs, if he attempted to use her ill. —And to impress his menace more strongly, he was often seen, from the parlour windows, swaggering about the park with his hat fiercely cocked, and a long sword by his side, as if he was ready to be called in on the first summons.

No poor wretch was ever so miserably harrassed, as Sir James. His misfortunes, (or rather his *distresses*, for they were all of his own bringing on) had now sunk his spirits, and totally

totally unmanned him. He needed not such a spectre always before his windows to keep him within. Duns, and writs, and jails, were frightful ideas, and always in his thoughts. If he went to the door, he feared a bailiff in every bush.—As to the affair of the woman, he determined to make up matters as well as he could; and submit again to that tyranny, which he could not throw off; tho he feared it would now be more insufferable than ever.

In no very short time, however he was relieved, as far as getting rid of this nuisance could relieve him.
While

While she lived with him, tho totally negligent of *his* affairs, she had been very intent on *her own:* and had secured a good purse for herself; which in the wreck of his fortune, she found no very difficult matter. But when she now saw there was nothing more to be had, she had no inclination to stay longer; and took an opportunity early one morning to disappear, carrying the family-jewels with her, (which she would never suffer him to dispose of) and what else of value she could easily pack up. Her brother waited for her with a chaise at the
park-

park-gate; and where they went, nobody could tell.

The next day however Sir James received a note from her, intimating, that, "As she found he had lost all af-
"fection for her, she would no longer
"diſtreſs him with her preſence.
"Nor would she intrude farther on
"his bounty. The little things he
"had given her, would ſufficiently
"maintain her: only she begged, he
"would, for her ſake, take a fatherly
"care of the poor children she had
"left him."—Three of them, now young women, (poor uneducated creatures) were growing up to be as

great

great plagues, as their mother had been. What to do with them; and what to do with himself, were matters of diſtraction to him.

But the jewels were his firſt concern. As they were very valuable, and what he had looked on as his laſt ſtake, he determined to purſue her with a warrant. But his attorney told him, that conſidering how things had been circumſtanced between them, and that ſhe had often been ſeen with thoſe jewels about her in public, he much doubted, whether he could recover them, even if he ſhould be able

to

to find her. He was obliged therefore to defift.

At length, having fold his laft unfettled acre, and collected from the wreck of his affairs, all he could, he gave his poor girls little more than was juft fufficient to keep them from ftarving; and with the reft, he endeavoured to find a refuge abroad from the diftreffes he fuffered at home.

All thefe evils he had brought upon himfelf, together with the total ruin of his conftitution, before he had attained the age of forty-feven. What became of him afterwards, was never

never certainly known: but it was commonly suppofed, he ended his days in fome obfcure part of Italy, or Switzerland.

During the feveral years, that Sir James Leigh was thus harraffed with an imperious woman, whom he detefted, but could not fhake off, Mr. Willoughby was enjoying the full happinefs of domeftic comfort. He had married a lady every way deferving of him. They had but one mind between them, which was centered in making each other happy; and in diffufing happinefs, as far as they could, around

around them. The first object of their care was the education of their little family; and they had the satisfaction to see them grow up with every hopeful appearance.

As their eldest son advanced towards manhood, the old people of the parish used to say, he put them much in mind of what his father had been at his age. He was the same engaging youth, with his auburn hair hanging in curls about his shoulders—modest, civil, and obliging to every body; and most pleased, when he had the power given him of pleasing others.

He

He married, as his father had done, early in life; and equally to the satisfaction of his parents. On this event his father settled an estate of two thousand a year upon him; and put him in possession of that house, which his grandmother had formerly occupied.

Mr. Willoughby was now happy in his grandchildren. Seldom a day passed, in which two or three of them did not come to play upon the lawn, before his study-windows; and would run in, one at a time, to deliver some message from mama; or to ask for one of his sticks to ride upon.

Mr.

Mr. Willoughby lived many years after his son's marriage, with a greater share of felicity, than happens to most men. He was happy in himself—in his fame—in his fortunes—in his children—and above all, in his excellent Lucy, who doubled all his pleasures—divided all his cares—and lessened all his pains.

THE END.

MEMOIRS

OF

JOHN WILMOT,

Earl of Rochester.

JOHN WILMOT, Earl of Rochester, in Charles the second's reign, poſſeſſed more the graces of an elegant perſon—was better bred—and was more lively and agreeable in converſation, than almoſt any man of his time. While his manners made him univerſally engaging; his parts and knowledge introduced him to men of genius, and letters. He was fond of reading; and found one of his greateſt pleaſures to ariſe from in-
creaſing

creasing his knowledge. His dispofition too was naturally good. He was well natured, obliging to every body, and never backward in serving a friend.

He finished his education abroad, under the conduct of a very worthy tutor: and brought home with him a greater variety of just observations on men, and things, than most young men are able to collect.

To his other accomplishments he added the splendor of military glory; having served twice with the Earl of Sandwich, as a volunteer in the Dutch war, with great reputation.—And

what

what gave a polish to all his accomplishments and good qualities, was the unassuming modesty of his behaviour. He himself was the only person who appeared unconscious of the superiority of his parts and knowledge.

Thus qualified, he was fatally introduced to the licentious court of Charles the second, who made him one of the gentlemen of his bedchamber, and ranger of Woodstock park.

The life of a courtier gave a new turn to his ideas. He became the idol of all the gay, the profligate, and unprincipled young people, with whom that court abounded. His manners were so engaging, and his wit, and humour so entertaining, especially when a little inlivened with wine, that he was continually beset by 'those, who watched every opportunity of enjoying his company.

Tho Lord Rochester had a taste for literature, he soon also felt a taste for pleasure, which in the end destroyed every principle of virtue.—In the early part of his life he had a relish only for the company of men of genius, sense, and learning. But court manners rendered him less nice. He was frequently obliged to mix with trifling, illiterate, and vicious people: and

finding

finding he could unbend himself among them, and be perfectly at his ease; he began to find a relish in their company; and by degrees to like no other company so well.

Thus entered among profligate people, he soon became eminent. As he was superior to all his companions in wit and genius, he soon outdid them all likewise in every kind of depravity. He gave a loose to his appetites, and courted pleasure in every form. During five years of his life, he confessed, he was hardly ever in such a state as could be called perfectly sober; and in this time was guilty of a

thou-

thousand strange extravagancies. He would go about the country in various shapes, seldom without some profligate intention—chiefly in pursuit of some low amour. But whatever character he assumed—a farmer—a sailor—a razor-grinder—a beggar—or any other—he acted his part in every disguise, so incomparably well, that if he had met even an intimate friend, as he frequently did, he would pass undiscovered; and would afterwards tell his friend some circumstances of his life, which the other thought he only could have known by witchcraft. Once being obliged to keep out of the way,

he

he became a mountebank on Tower-hill; and was enough acquainted with phyfic, to delude the populace into an opinion of his wonderful abilities. In this profeffion, he ufed to fay, he could have made a very comfortable fubfiftence, if he had wifhed it.

Nor was he more abandoned to the indulgence of his appetites, than loofe to every principle of common honefty. Pleafure was his only purfuit. This led him into expence. Expence produced neceffity; and neceffity, difhonefty. Profeffions of friendfhip to thofe whom he mortally hated, and intended, if he could, to ruin—un-

meaning

meaning oaths and vows in his addresses to women—tricks put upon tradesmen, and creditors, to deceive, and cheat them, with a variety of other dishonest practices, were common with him. In short, no man ever gave himself up to pleasure with more eagerness—was less restrained by principle in the pursuit of it—was better qualified to procure it—or had a higher relish for the enjoyment of it when procured.

But one great obstacle still obtruded itself on these joyous pursuits. Tho' he had not principle enough to restrain his actions, he had enough to alarm

alarm his conscience. Mere morality he was able to manage pretty well; were it not for its inconvenient connection with religion. It was necessary for him therefore to reason down all the troublesome reflections, which arose on this subject; and with this view he had gotten together all the common-place arguments he could invent, or collect—many of them taken up from those, whom on any other subject he would have despised.

It cannot be supposed, that a mind so full of intelligence as his was, could easily be divested of every idea of religion. The being of a God he allowed.

lowed. He said, he never could conceive the world to be made by chance; the productions and regularity of nature, proclaimed beyond contradiction an infinite power. But then he wished to infer from various circumstances, which he did not care to examine deeply, that this power had little concern with the affairs of men. He could not, he said, attribute human passions—hate, or love—to a perfect being. That would be to form a Deity on heathen theology: and therefore, where there was neither love nor hatred, he could not suppose

there

there could be either reward, or punishment.

Then again he thought, that to love God, was presumptuous—to fear him, superstitious. Prayer he thought could be of no use, as it was not to be imagined the Deity was so weak, as to be wrought on by the importunities of man. All religious worship therefore, except, as he would say, in a gay humour, a few hymns in celebration of the divine majesty, he supposed to be useless.

Two maxims in morality he confessed he could not but hold, however little he had lived up to them.—That
we

we should do nothing to injure another; nor any thing to prejudice ourselves—particularly our own health: but that the gratification of our appetites, when it did not interfere with either of these points, he endeavoured to persuade himself was very lawful. It was unreasonable he thought to suppose they were put into man, merely to be restrained.

It was his favourite doctrine, that self-interest governed the world; and that it was right it should do so. What was general benevolence, he would ask, but putting one man's happiness in the power of another?
Whereas,

Whereas, if every man took care of himself, the business was in safer hands, and the end would be better answered.

Still however the doctrine of a future state recurred, notwithstanding all his endeavours to stifle it; and was more in his way than any thing else; as he could not believe the soul would be dissolved by death. What might become of it, he could not pretend to say: but still he persuaded himself the doctrine of rewards and punishments was not included in its immortality. That doctrine, he wished to believe, was big with absurdity. Heaven appeared

peared to him too good for the best; and hell too bad for the worst. And indeed he conceived, if God was the good Being he was represented, he could not, consistently with that goodness, make any of his creatures miserable.

Thus he had formed a sort of religion for himself which he had contrived to answer an unprincipled life. As for the religion of the bible, he found it of too rigid a texture to mold into any commodious form. He was obliged therefore to strike the bible entirely out of his scheme. In order to this, like other infidels, he would
listen

listen to no *evidence* in its favour; but thought every *objection*, tho he might have found it answered over and over, highly worth his attention.

As for the inspiration of the scriptures, he used to say, he knew not what it meant. He could not conceive, how God should reveal his secrets to men. Nor indeed could he see any occasion for revealed religion at all, as he had no idea of man's having been ever placed in a better state than he was in at present. And even if a revelation had been necessary, one should have thought it would have been more extensive; and have taken
place

place long before the time of Augustus Cæsar.—As to prophecies, and miracles, the world had ever been full of such wonderful stories—and he supposed they all depended intirely on the credulity and folly of mankind.—The scriptures, he thought, carried on their very face the marks of imposition: the stile and manner of writing—the various contradictions, which he found in them—the disorder in point of time—and many other things, he owned, had sufficient weight with him to destroy their credibility.—Besides, he said if a man *could not believe*, which was his case, faith could neither be be *forced* upon him, nor *required*—and the mysteries of scripture, such as the trinity—the incarnation—the atonement, and some others, were to him wholly incomprehensible.

But of all things, he plumed his infidelity most upon the bad lives of the professors of christianity. As the clergyman, he said, had studied religion, he must of course be best acquainted with the evidences of it: and if these evidences had no effect on him, it was shrewdly to be suspected, there was no weight in them. When he saw clergymen therefore at court, using so many mean arts, as he often did, in obtaining preferment, he could not suppose, they conceived better of the christian religion, than he himself did.

Thus we have taken a short view of the abandoned life of this uncommonly wicked profligate. We have seen the pleas he made use of to cover his vices; and the arguments he used with himself, such as they were, to strengthen his infidelity. His whole life indeed was only a struggle against conviction: for a man of his sense could not avoid perceiving that when he debased religion, he put a force

upon

upon nature.—Let us now fee the end of all this: and how it concluded at length in the triumph of religion.

Whilft this noble profligate enjoyed his health, and met with no checks from nature in the purfuit of pleafure, all was well. His mind was occupied in a thoufand pleafureable engagements—reflection was turned afide—and his confcience in a great degree filenced.——But vicious enjoyments have feldom an extended date. Before he had attained his thirtieth year, Lord Rochefter had out-run his conftitution; and found every accefs of pleafure to be an accefs alfo of difeafe.

case. He was now worn down to a shadow; and confumptive symptoms were increafing daily upon him. But what threatened the moft immediate danger, was an ulcer, which his phyficians thought was forming in his bladder. As it gave him however no great uneafinefs, he hoped it might difperfe without any fatal effects. And indeed he found himfelf afterwards fo well, that having occafion to vifit his eftate in Somerfetfhire, he undertook the journey with his ufual impetuofity, and rode poft. But the heat, and violence of the exercife fo inflamed the ulcer, which might probably

bly with care and quietnefs, have difperfed, that he was obliged to return in his coach to Woodftock-lodge, very much out of order.

God affords all finners *opportunities of reflection*—fome circumftances in each man's life, which, if they were as properly accepted, as they are gracioufly intended, would lead him to repentance. Some men are drawn by cords of love. But fevere calamities only can bring others to reflection. When they feel the world failing under them; and its beft promifes ending in deceit, if they are not hardened

ened beyond all reflection, they naturally look round for something that can administer comfort.

This was the case of the Earl of Rochester. He had lived a pleasureable, and a vicious life. The pleasure was now gone, the remembrance of the wickedness alone was left. It shocked him to think he had given up his health, his fortune, his friends, his character—every thing in this world that was valuable, for what he now only remembered with horror.

But this was so far mere worldly compunction. It led however to more serious reflection.—As this world

world failed, the next drew nearer: and as he always had some conception of a future state, tho he wished not to suppose it a state of retribution, his active mind could not help being anxious for better information. He knew he had never examined into these matters with any attention himself; and therefore could not but doubt his own crude reasonings, which never could amount to more than mere conjecture. His friends therefore, particularly his mother, the Countess Dowager of Rochester, endeavoured to get serious people about him: hoping they might put thoughts

into

into his mind, which his own active-spirit would easily pursue.—Among, these, the chief were Mr. Parsons, her chaplain—and Dr. Burnet, afterwards bishop of Salisbury. One or other of these was frequently with him, and by degrees he took pleasure in their conversation. To Dr. Burnet he shewed a particular attachment; and desired him on his death-bed, to give the world an account of the conversations that passed between them. "I have done much mischief, said he, in my life-time; I should wish to make some amends for it at my death."

To

To these two gentlemen Lord Rochester laid open, without scruple, all the vile opinions he had held in the early part of his life. He never, he said, was satisfied with them. He always felt strong remorse of conscience; tho too often, he feared it was founded on his having ruined himself in this world. Yet sometimes he believed the disequietude of his mind had a better principle. "I remember once;
" said he, at the house of a person of
" quality, where several of us pro-
" phane young fellows had met toge-
" ther, I undertook the cause of
" atheism: and I was thought to have
" per-

"performed my part so well, that I
"was overwhelmed with applause.
"But as I left the company, I felt
"myself exceedingly shocked at what
"had passed; and could not help
"breaking out into some such solilo-
"quy as this—Good Heavens! that
"a man, who walks upright—who
"sees around him the wonderful
"works of God—and has the use of
"his senses and reason—could ever
"abuse them in so horridly prophane
"a manner!". Indeed, he would say,
in the worst part of his life, he never
could, with all his reasoning, persuade
himself into atheism. He was something

thing like the devils: he *believed and trembled.*

At other times he would confess, that notwithstanding his own licentious actions, he always felt a secret value for an honest man; and always thought morality sat well on others. But he owned he had never felt any reverence for the gospel—nor had ever taken that pains in seeking into its evidence, which a matter of that *apparent* importance required.— The first thing, he told Dr. Burnet, which made him think seriously of christianity, was a conversation he had with Mr. Parsons; who speaking of pro-

prophecy, pointed out to him the fifty-third chapter of Isaiah; and shewed him how exactly the sufferings of our Saviour described there, agreed with the account given of them by the evangelists; tho it is certain the book of Isaiah was written many ages before our Saviour lived, and is esteemed by the Jews at this day to be divinely inspired. This comparison so intirely satisfied his understanding, that the passion of our Saviour he said, appeared as clear and plain to to him, as any object he ever saw re-presented in a glass. The original, and the image were exactly alike.—This passage

paſſage from Iſaiah he got by heart, and frequently ſoothed himſelf by repeating it.

And here let us pauſe a moment. As God affords all ſinners *opportunities of reflection,* ſo does he likewiſe afford them various *means of converſion,* according to their various diſpoſitions, and different modes of thinking. One man is ſtruck with the wonderful works of God. The imagination of another faſtens on ſome beautiful analogy of nature. A third is awakened by ſome pious life he has read—or ſome ſermon he has heard

heard—or conversation that has struck him. A fourth is affected by the simplicity, and purity of scriptural precepts, or examples. From one or other of these sources, or something else perhaps in the divine economy, which forcibly strikes his mind, the sinner will often through the grace of God assisting his pious endeavours, take the beginning of a new life.—Lord Rochester we have seen, was first brought to a sense of religion by the wonderful coincidence between the prophecies and the history of Christ.

Having thus gained as it were, a glimpse of christianity, his intuitive mind

mind eafily proceeded. From fimply contemplating the fufferings of Chrift, he began to inquire into the caufe of thofe fufferings. He faw in a ftrong light his own wicked life, and the heinoufnefs of fin; and devoutly acknowledged the neceffity of a Redeemer. "O bleffed God! he "would cry, can fuch a creature as "I have been, gain acceptance from "thee! Can there be any mercy for "me! Will God own fuch a wretch! "—Never, never, he would add, but "through the infinite merits of a Re- "deemer—never, but by the pur- "chafe of his blood."—Then again, a fenfe a sense of his own guilt flowing in strongly upon him, he would cry out, (striking his hands together) he had been the vilest dog, the sun ever shone upon: and thought the life of a starving leper, crawling in a ditch, as he expressed himself, more enviable than a life like his.

In short, his whole frame being thus intirely changed, he carried into religion all those strong feelings, and warm passions, which had led him so violently astray in the paths of vice.

- In a calmer interval, he would speak of the foolish, and absurd philosophy of the late Mr. Hobbes, and others

others of that stamp. "Aye, he would cry, these were my ruin. These philosophers helped to undo me."

Then laying his hand on the bible, he would say, " *There* is true philosophy.—This is the wisdom that speaks to the heart. A *bad life*, is the only grand objection to this book. And it is surely a bad way in examining the truth of it, to *begin with cavilling*. Let us examine first th *evidence* and *tendency* of it, and try whether that will not blunt the edge of many *objections*."

In short, christianity had taken such full possession of his mind, that

altho

altho he had been at first awakened from his criminal life by dreadful apprehensions, and horrors, his conversion was now founded on a firm belief of the gospel; his mind became daily more calm; and he prayed to God with all earnestness for his grace and holy spirit to assist him in keeping steady to the resolutions he had formed.—In his devotions, he would sometimes use his own prayers; which Mr. Parsons, who was often with him at prayer, used to say, were truly excellent.

As his heart seemed thus changed,
the

the habits of his life were changed with it,

He was very folicitous to have all his debts paid; many of which he had contracted without any defign of paying them at all.

Acts of reftitution alfo he ordered, when reftitution was in his power. When it was not, he prayed to God earneftly to forgive him, and mercifully to accept a fincere intention.

The thoughts of his corrupt writings gave him great diftrefs. They could not be recalled: but he hoped, that whoever heard of them, would hear alfo of the diftrefs they had given him.

him. Such of his writings however, as were unpublished—all his lascivious pictures—and every thing else that had a bad tendency, he strictly ordered his executors to burn.

Injuries which he had received himself, many of them great, and provoking, he declared in the presence of God, he forgave from his heart; and was ready to do any act of kindness in his power, to those who had offended him.

He had formerly indulged such a habit of swearing, that oaths made a part of his common conversation: and when he was heated, they were frightful.

frightful. But he had now so wholly mastered this vile habit, that bishop Burnet tells us, when fits of pain came upon him, which were frequent, and violent, he never heard any thing like an oath escape him. On one occasion indeed, when he was suffering under an acute paroxysm of his disorder, and had sent a servant for something, which he thought he might have brought sooner, he cried out, " That d———d fellow I suppose is lost." When the bishop remarked it, he said, " Aye, you see how this lan-
" guage of fiends still hangs about me
" —Who deserves d———g so much as

"myself?—God forgive me!"—Except on this occasion, the bishop observes, he never heard even a hasty expression come from him. To his servants indeed, during his whole illness, he was kind, considerate, and even affectionate; giving them as little trouble as he could help; and apologizing for every extraordinary trouble he was obliged to put upon them.——His regard for them he still shewed more effectually in his will.

Among his other faults, he had shewn much unkindness to his relations. He had paid little respect to his mother—he had neglected his Lady; and

and been inattentive to his children. His behaviour in all these instances, was now wholly changed. To his mother it was respectful in the greatest degree—to his Lady, tender and affectionate. She was a very amiable woman; and having been recovered from the church of Rome, in which she had been brought up, it gave him, he said, unspeakable satisfaction to receive the holy sacrament with her, from the hands of a protestant clergyman.—Her gentle attention to him in his illness, which was unwearied, filled him with the tenderest remorse, and a thousand nameless sensibilities.—For

his

his children's happiness he seemed highly concerned. He had a son, and three daughters; and would often call them to him, and speak to them in so affecting a manner, as no words but his own, could express. Once as the bishop was sitting by him, when his children were with him, he cried out, " See how good, God has been to me in giving me so many blessings— What an ungracious dog have I been!"

On another occasion, speaking of the great concern he was under for their pious education, he earnestly hoped his son would never be a wit—
that

that is, said he, one of those wretched beings, who pride themselves in scoffing at God, and religion. An honest and religious man, he added, is a character, beyond any thing fortune, and honours have to give. He then blessed them, and prayed for them; and committed them to the protection of God.

It was a favourite topic with him, whenever he had opportunity, to set himself up as a melancholy example to deter others from a bad life.—A gentlemen of some quality called, one day to see him. "Aye, look at me, "said Lord Rochester, and see what
"a man

"a man is reduced to, who has
"spent his life in scoffing at God, and
"religion. You and I, my good
"friend, have been old sinners toge-
"ther; and therefore I am the more
"free with you. I hope you will see
"your wickedness, as I have seen
"mine. Depend upon it, my friend,
"we have been mistaken in our con-
"ceits. Our opinions are ill-found-
"ed. Therefore may God grant you
"repentance!"

Bishop Burnet also tells us, that Lord Rochester gave it to him in charge, a little before his death, to tell a certain person from him, for whose wel-

welfare he was much concerned; that altho there were nothing to come, after this life; yet all the pleasures he had ever known in sin, would have been ill bought with half the torture he had felt on the recollection of them.

Thus this noble Lord had done much in a little time. His sins had been great: his repentance was severe: and, as his hours shortened, he became perfectly composed; and expressed a willingness, and even a wish to die. He hoped he should never relapse, if God should grant him a longer life: but he thought he could never expect to

to be in a better ſtate to die, than he was in at that time. "And indeed,
" ſays biſhop Burnet, I had every
" reaſon to believe him perfectly ſin-
" cere. I remember, continues the
" biſhop, after his having had many
" ſleepleſs nights, a doſe of laudanum
" was adminiſtered to him without
" his knowledge. The effect of it
" was a moſt refreſhing ſleep. In the
" morning he found himſelf ſo per-
" fectly well, that he thought his diſ-
" order was now come to a criſis; and
" that nothing ailed him, but weak-
" neſs, which he ſuppoſed would in a
" little time go off. As he was fully
poſſeſſed

"possessed with this idea, he enter-
"tained me with the scheme of his
"future life. He would retire from
"the world, he said, and spend the
"remainder of his days, in study, in-
"nocence, and piety." And the
bishop had no doubt but he was sincere; and that if he had lived, he
would have put all this in execution.
The joys of religion seemed to have
taken so much hold of him, that it
was not likely he would ever again
have given them up for the pleasures
of sin.

But this relaxation from pain was
soon over. When the refreshment of
the

the night went off, it left him in the fame ſtate in which it found him. Two days longer he languiſhed.— But nature was now entirely exhauſted. The diſcharge from the ulcer was ſo great, that his whole body was in a manner, conſumed. He was frequently alſo in violent pain: and from lying ſo long in one poſture, the depreſſed parts began to mortify. Notwithſtanding however all this diſtreſs, his compoſure, and reſignation were wonderful. He ſpoke little—was heard to pray fervently; and on the 26th of July, 1680, in the thirty-third year of his age, he died at Woodſtock-park in in Oxfordshire.—About a month before he died, he dictated the following paper, which he signed with his own hand; and had it regularly attested.

"*For the benefit of all those, whom I may have drawn into sin by my example, and encouragement, I leave to the world this my last declaration, which I deliver in the presence of the great God, who knows the secrets of all hearts, and before whom I am now appearing to be judged——that from the bottom of my soul, I detest and abhor the whole course of my former wicked life; and that I think I can never sufficiently admire*

admire the goodness of God, who has given me a true sense of the pernicious opinions, and vile practices, in which I have hitherto lived without hope, and without God in the world—having been an open enemy to Jesus Christ, and doing the utmost despight to the holy spirit of grace——and that the greatest testimony of my charity to such is, to warn them in the name of God, and as they regard the welfare of their immortal souls, no more to deny his being, or his providence, or despise his goodness—no more to make a mock of sin, or contemn the pure and excellent religion of my ever blessed Redeemer,

through

through whose merits alone, I, one of the greatest of sinners, do yet hope for mercy and forgiveness. Amen.

Rochester.

Declared, and signed, June the 19th, 1680, in the presence of

>Anne Rochester.
>Robert Parsons.

Such was the life of this very extraordinary man. It resolves itself into three distinct periods—each, in its way equally wonderful. In the first, he appeared in the polite world, as the most accomplished gentleman of his time. In the second, he became the most abandoned profligate: and in the last, the most sincere penitent.

What a happy man might he have been, if he could have kept his desires within the bounds of virtue, and have added religion to the blessings he enjoyed! He had every thing that the world could give: but grasping at pleasure in excess, he found it misery. A harrassed mind, and a diseased body were the fruits of his vicious pleasures—the loss of every worldly enjoyment—and at a period,.

when life is in its prime, the decrepitude of age.

He had the wisdom however at last to turn his sufferings to account; and see his errors, before it was too late. But what remorse, horror, and anguish did it cost him, before he arrived at that peaceful serenity, which he might with innocence have enjoyed to a late period of life.

Some are inclined, through zeal for the honour of God, to take from the force of these extraordinary conversions, by supposing, that God arbitrarily vouchsafes a peculiar influx of his grace to one man, which he denies to another—that we have nothing therefore to do in the work of such conversions ourselves: they are the entire work of God; and the greater the sinner the more abundant often is the grace.

No doubt, it is a doctrine of scripture, that all our goodness is derived from God: but it is the doctrine of scripture also that our own endeavours must co-operate with God's goodness, and make his grace effectual. When we are told that *God worketh in us both to will, and to do of his good pleasure;* that is, through his good pleasure that he worketh in us, us at all; we are told alfo, that *we are to work out our own falvation with fear and trembling.* Every opinion therefore, however well-meant, which has a *tendency* to check our own pious endeavours; and to lay the *whole work*, if I may fo fpeak, on God, appears to be equally unfcriptural, and mifchievous.

St. Paul's cafe is mentioned, and that of the thief on the crofs, as inftances of fudden, and peculiar effufions of grace. But neither of them feems to be a cafe in point. St. Paul was a man of great piety. His difpofition was always good; and his practice agreeable to what he thought the will of God. He was only under a violent prejudice, which it pleased God to remove by an *open miracle.*

As to the thief on the cross, we may suppose he had then the first *religious opportunity* he had ever had—and that the sight of his suffering Saviour wrought in him at once a full conviction. The history does not give us the least ground for more, or to believe he received any *peculiar* interference of grace, which was denied to his companion.

In short, we are *not* told in what *manner* the grace of God co-operates with man. But we *are* told, that
God

'God is *no respecter of persons*: and every part of scripture injoins us the practice of a holy life founded on our faith in Christ.

Others again, who are less concerned about religion, would take from the force of such conversions, as this of Lord Rochester, by attributing them to a melancholy oppression of spirits; or by resolving them into enthusiasm or superstition. But why should any of these causes be assigned to Lord Rochester's conversion? Does it appear from the history of his life that he was under any oppression of spirits—that he was under any fear, but what was the effect of guilt—which is the very medium of every conversion; and which all wicked men must feel, before they can be brought to a sense of their wickedness?—Does it appear, that there was any thing enthusiastic, or superstitious in his ideas of christianity? and particularly, in his declaration at his death?—or in short, does it appear that he held any opinion, which all sober christians do not, at all times hold? If so; why should we attribute to a bad cause, what has the fairest pretensions to the best?

Be-

Besides, all who were about Lord Rochester at the time of his death, speak of his faculties as perfectly lucid, and equal to what they had ever been. Bishop Burnet perhaps takes more than ordinary pains to wipe off any supposition, that at the time of his death, he was under any particular weakness of imagination; and speaks of the great vivacity of his discourse, which was equal at that time, to what he had ever observed in the days of his most perfect health.

THE END.

MEMOIRS

OF

NAIMBANNA,

A

Young African Prince.

WHEN the Sierra Leone company were first settled, they endeavoured to bring over to their friendship all the petty African princes in their neighbourhood. Among others, they applied to a chief, of the name of Naimbanna, who was remarkable for a good disposition, and an acute understanding. He easily saw the intention of the company was friendly to Africa, and entered into amity with them.

They

They spoke to him about the slave-trade, and gave him reasons for wishing to have it abolished. He was convinced of its vileness; and declared, that not one of his subjects should ever go into slavery again.

By degrees they began to talk to him about religion. But he was rather wary on that head. It seems he had received a prejudice against christianity, from the following circumstance.

The Portugueze had, at that time, several missionaries about the country, who under the pretence of preaching christianity, sold charms to the natives;

tives; and in exchange received ivory, gold duſt, and other commodities for the merchants, by whom they were employed. Among their converts, was one of Naimbanna's chief friends; who had afterwards many converſations with Naimbanna on the ſubject of religion; and endeavoured to make a convert of him alſo. He told Naimbanna, that the chriſtian religion was the beſt religion in the world; for a man could do nothing ſo bad, which the prieſts of that religion would not forgive for a mere trifle. Naimbanna with great acuteneſs of mind, told him,

he

he thought a good religion would never suffer that; and refused to be a chriſtian. On talking therefore with the gentlemen of the factory, on this ſubject, and finding they profeſſed chriſtianity, as well as the Portugueze miſſionaries, he concluded their tenets were the ſame, and paid little attention to them.

By degrees however he found, that the factory contained a very good ſort of people—that they lived happily among themſelves, and did not ſell pardons for gold duſt as the Portugueze did. He began therefore to think more favourably both of them and their religion.

But

But tho it appears he had a much juster opinion of chriſtianity, than he had received from the Portugueze miſſionaries; yet he was ſtill backward either in receiving it himſelf, or in making it the religion of his country. He was well convinced of the barbarous ſtate of his own people, on a compariſon with Europeans, and wiſhed for nothing more than a reformation among them—eſpecially in religion. But as he found there were ſeveral kinds of religion in the world, he wiſhed to know which was the beſt, before he introduced any.

N To

To ascertain this point as well as he could, he took the following method. He sent one of his sons into Turkey, among the Mahometans—a second into Portugal, among the papists; supposing probably that the missionaries did not teach their religion properly—and a third he recommended to the Sierra Leone company, desiring they would send him into England, to be there instructed in the religion of the country. By the report of his sons, it appears, he meant to be directed in the choice of a national religion.

Of the two former of these young men we have no particulars; only that

that one of them became very vicious. It is the laſt mentioned, tho, I believe, the eldeſt, who bore his father's name, Naimbanna, to whom this account belongs. The Sierra Leone company received the charge of him with great pleaſure, believing that nothing could have a better effect in promoting their benevolent ſchemes, than making him a good chriſtian.

Young Naimbanna was a perfect African in his form. He was black, had woolly hair, thick lips, and that blunt ſingularity of feature, with which the African face is commonly marked. While he was with the company, he seemed a well-disposed, tractable youth; but when opposed, impatient, fierce, and subject to violent passions.

In the first ship that sailed, he was sent to England, where he arrived in the year 1791. We may imagine with what astonishment he surveyed every object that came before him: but his curiosity in prudent hands became from the first, the medium of useful instruction.

During his voyage he had picked up a little of the English language; to which he was not a perfect stranger when he embarked. He had gotten

hold

hold of several words and phrases; and tho he could not speak it with any degree of fluency, he could understand much of what he heard spoken; which greatly facilitated his learning it, when he came to it in a more regular way.

The difficulty of learning to speak, and read, being in a great degree subdued, he was put upon the grand point, for which he was sent into England——that of being instructed in the christian religion. The gentlemen to whose care he had been recommended, alternately took him under their protection; and each gave up his

his whole time to him, faithfully discharging the trust he had voluntarily, and without any emolument undertaken.

Naimbanna was first convinced that the bible was the word of God; the most material parts of which—of the old testament, as well as of the new—were explained to him. The great necessity of a Saviour from the sinfulness of man was pointed out—the end and design of christianity—its doctrines—its precepts, and its sanctions, were all made intelligible to him. With a clearness of understanding, which astonished those who took the

care

care of inſtructing him, he made theſe divine truths familiar to him: and having no prejudices to oppoſe, but the abſurdities of his own country, which were eaſily ſubdued, he received the goſpel with joy; and carried it home to his heart as the means of happineſs both in this world and the next.

His love for reading the ſcriptures, and hearing them read, was ſuch, that he was never tired of the exerciſe.*

---

* Mrs. H. More, who knew him well, informed the author, that altho ſhe never ſaw Naimbanna fatigued with this exerciſe, he had often fatigued her with reading the ſcripture at his deſire inceſſantly to him.

Every other part of learning that he was put upon, as arithmetic for inſtance, was heavy work with him; and he ſoon began to complain of fatigue: but even when he was moſt fatigued, if he was aſked to read in the bible, he was always ready; and generally expreſſed his readineſs by ſome emotions of joy. In ſhort, he conſidered the bible as the rule which was to direct his life; and he made a real uſe of every piece of inſtruction he obtained from it. This was evident in all his actions. If his behaviour was at any time wrong, and a paſſage of ſcripture was ſhewn to him, which for-

forbad the impropriety or wrong behaviour, whatever it was, he inftantly complied with the rule he received. Of this there were many inftances.

One related to drefs. He had a little touch of vanity about him—was fond of finery—admired it in other people, and was always ready to adorn himfelf. His kind inftructors told him thefe were childifh inclinations—that decency, and propriety of drefs were pleafing: but that foppery was difgufting. Above all, they told him the fcripture idea was very different. The chriftian was ordered to be *cloathed with humility;* and to put on the

orna-

ornament of a *meek and quiet spirit.* Such passages, whenever they were suggested to him, checked all the little vanities of his heart; and made him ashamed of what he had just before so eagerly desired.

The irritable passions, where lay his weakest side, were conquered in the same way. His friends once carried him to the house of commons to hear a debate on the slave trade; which colonel Tarlton defended with some warmth. When Naimbanna came out of the house, he exclaimed with great vehemence and indignation, that he would kill that man where-ever

ever he met him; for he told stories of his country. He told people that his countrymen would not work; and that was a great story. His countrymen would work; but Englishmen would not buy work; they would buy only men.—His friends told him, he should not be so angry with colonel Tarlton; for perhaps he had been misinformed, and knew no better. Besides they told him, that at any rate, he had no right to kill him; for God says, *Vengeance is mine, I will repay, saith the Lord.* This calmed him in a moment: and he never afterwards expressed the least indignation

at

at colonel Tarlton; but would have been ready to have shewn him any friendly office, if it had fallen in his way.

At another time, when he saw a drayman using his horse ill; he fired at it exceedingly; and declared in a violent passion, he would get a gun, and shoot that fellow directly. He would always, he said, carry a gun about him to kill such sort of people, for they deserved to be killed. But his anger was presently asswaged, by some such passage from scripture, as, *Be ye angry and sin not: let not the sun go down upon your wrath.*

Among

Among the difficulties, in which his new religion involved him, one respected his wives. He had married three; but he clearly saw the new testament allowed only one. What should he do with the other two? Then again, if he should repudiate two of them, which should he retain? In justice he thought he should keep her, whom he had married first. But she was not the wife of his affections. He loved the second best. In short, he shewed so much tenderness of conscience on this, and every other point, that he seemed anxious about nothing, but *to know what his religion required him*

him to do. When he could determine the *rectitude* of an action, he set an example to christians, by shewing he thought there was no difficulty in the *performance.* Whether he met with any casuist, to set him right in the matter of his wives, I never heard. It is certain however, that while he continued in England, he shewed no sign, in any instance, of infidelity to his African engagements.

With regard to liquor, which is a great temptation to an African, he was, from the first, perfectly sober. He said, his father had ordered him never to drink more at a time than a single

single glass of wine, when he came into England; and he considered his father's injunction as sacred. It was probably founded on the knowledge of his son's warmth of temper, which he feared wine might inflame. On this head therefore all the instruction he wanted, was to turn his temperance into a christian virtue, by practising it with a sincere desire to please God. .

Among the gay scenes, which Naimbanna could not but often see, he never mixed. His friends were very solicitous to keep him from all pleasurable dissipation, which might possibly have corrupted that beautiful simplicity

city of mind, which was so characteristic in him: tho indeed he never shewed a desire to join in any diversion, which they did not intirely approve. Dancing assemblies were the only meetings of amusement, for which he shewed the least inclination. But tho his friends were unwilling to trust him in any gay, promiscuous meetings of that kind, they were very ready to indulge him in a dance at home; and he enjoyed the exercise with great alacrity, jumping and capering, after the manner of his country, with an agility, which was too violent for any body but himself.—
He

He was fond alfo of riding on horfe-back; but when he got upon a horfe, there was no governing his defire of rapid motion.

He had now been a year and a half in England, and had been well inftructed in the chriftian religion, which he perfectly underftood. He was baptized therefore; and now only waited for the firft opportunity of going home, which did not happen till about five or fix months afterwards.

In the mean time two great points were the burthen of his thoughts, and gave

gave him much distress. The first related to his father, whose death, he had heard, had happened about a year after he left the country. The great cause of his solicitude was his uncertainty, whether his father had died a christian. He knew he had been well-disposed to christianity: but he had never heard, whether he had fully embraced it.

His other difficulty regarded himself. He had now attained the end he aimed at. He had been instructed in a religion, which, he was convinced, would promote the happiness of his people, if it could be established

among

among them. But how was that to be done? With regard to himself, he had had wife, and learned men to inftruct him. But what could his abilities do in fuch a work?—efpecially confidering the wild, and favage manners of his countrymen. In every light, the greatnefs of the attempt perplexed him.

With a mind diftreffed by thefe difficulties, he took an affectionate leave of his kind friends in England, and embarked for Africa in one of the company's fhips, which was named after him, the Naimbanna.

On the departure of this amiable youth, we cannot help sympathizing with his generous feelings on the state of his country, which all humane people must unite in deploring. Much do we admire the Sierra Leone company for their beneficent endeavours to rescue it from that miserable state of darkness, in which it is involved. But nothing perhaps places its wretched bondage in a more striking light, than such a character as we have just been exhibiting. When we were taught to believe the African had scarce a rank among human beings, it injured our feelings less to think of

the

the bafe condition to which he was reduced. But when we fee in him fuch inftances of fine affections—fuch generous fentiments—fuch aptitude to receive religious truth—and have every reafon to believe, that inftances of this kind are to be found, more or lefs, in all parts of this unhappy country; * what a fhocking idea does

---

* That a real, and general converfion of the negroes is no romantic project, but a thing perfectly practicable; and that it would be highly beneficial both to the flaves, and their proprietors, is evident from the progrefs already made in this work by the Moravian miffionaries. In the Danifh iflands of St. Thomas, St. Croix, and St. John,

does it prefent to fee all thefe fine feelings damped; and thoufands of thefe wretched fufferers, with all their generous propenfities about them, loft to themfelves—and to fociety—and dragged away into all the mifery, and abject neceffities, which follow flavery..

We

John, they have profelyted near 6,000 negroes. They have alfo a congregation of feveral thoufands in the ifland of Antigua; and I have been affured by a gentlemen of credit, who faw them at public worfhip, that their deportment was remarkably ferious, devout, amd edifying. And they fo greatly furpafs all the other flaves in fobriety, diligence, quietnefs, fidelity, and obedience, that the planters are anxious to have their negroes put under.

(199)

We left Naimbanna embarking for Africa, in a state of mind rather tending to despondency. He had too much sensibility about him to enjoy any settled repose. Tho he had always shewn great affection for his own country, and relations, yet the kindnesses he had received from his friends in England had impressed him

---

der the direction of the missionaries———See a note in the XVII. Sermon, Vol. I. of Bishop Porteus's Sermons,

We may suppose that the Africans are just as susceptible of these divine truths in a state of liberty, as in a state of slavery—and that the Moravian missionaries would be as well inclined to attend them in Africa, as in the West Indies.

strongly ;

strongly; and it was not without a great struggle with himself that he broke away from them at last.

The distress he felt was the greater, as the society he now mixed in at sea was very different from that he had left behind. The profligate manners, and licentious language of the ship's company, shocked him exceedingly. The purity of his mind could not bear it. He hoped in a christian country, he should always have found himself among christians. But he was greatly disappointed. The company he was in, appeared to him as ignorant, and uninformed as his

his own savage countrymen; and much less innocent in their manners. At length, the oaths, and abominable conversation he continually heard, disgusted him so much, that he complained to the captain of the ship, and desired him to put a stop to such indecent language. The captain endeavoured to check it; but with little effect; which gave Naimbanna new distress.

But what still more than all was the great burden of his mind, was the difficulty he foresaw in his attempt to introduce christianity among his countrymen. Many were the schemes he he thought of. But infuperable obftacles feemed to arife on every fide.

All this perplexity, which his active, and generous mind underwent, recoiled upon himfelf. His thoughts were continually on the ftretch; and, as it was thought, at length occafioned a fever, which feized him, as his voyage was nearly at an end. His malady increafing, was attended with a delirium, which left him only few lucid intervals. In thefe his mind always fhone out full of religious hope, and patient refignation to the will of God.

During

During one of these intervals he told Mr. Graham, (a fellow-passenger, with whom he was most intimate) that he began to think he should be called away, before he had an opportunity to tell his mother of the mercies of God towards him, and of his obligations to the Sierra Leone company. He then desired him to take pen and ink, and write his will. The will, as follows was written in the presence of captain Wooles, and of James Cato, a black servant, who attended Naimbanna. It was afterwards regretted, that Mr. Graham had not written the will exactly in the language, which

Naim-

Naimbanna dictated, instead of giving it a legal cast.

*On board the Naimbanna,
July 14, 1793.*

I, Henry Granville Naimbanna, having been, for some days, very unwell, and being apprehensive, that I may not reach my friends, have communicated the underwritten, in the presence of the subscribers.—It is my will, and desire, that my brother Bartholomew do pay to the Sierra Leone company thirteen tons of rice, or the value thereof, being in consideration of the sums expended by the said company on

my

my account.—And likewise, that my said brother shall pay the sum of fifty pounds sterling to Henry Thornton, Esq. for money advanced by him on my account.—It is my will also, that my brother Bartholomew shall possess all my estates, real, and personal, till my son Lewis shall be of age; and that he shall deliver unto my said son, all that he receives from me for him; and that he will always endeavour to be on a good understanding with the Sierra Leone company. I particularly request him, as far as he can, to oppose the slave trade; and that nothing injurious may be imputed to the Sierra Leone company by by any evil-minded men, whose interest may be to oppose that worthy company.—I here declare in the presence of that God, in whom I place my trust, that during my stay in England, I always enjoyed very good health; and received the greatest kindness from all those, whose care I was under; and that, at my leaving England, I was in perfect health.—It is likewise my request, that my brother shall send to the Suzee country for the cows, that belonged to my father; and that he will present three of them to the governor and council of the Sierra Leone company. And if he does not find that number of cows, that he will

will purchase three others, and give them in my name.—I farther defire, that my brother will pay James Dean Cato, who attended me as my fervant, the fum of five bars.——

When Mr. Graham had written thus far, Naimbanna complained of fatigue; and faid, he would finifh his will after he had taken a little reft. But foon after, his fever came on with increafed violence, and his delirium fcarce ever left him afterwards.

In this will, we fee the workings of his generous mind, which feems chiefly to have been intent on two things—

things—the remuneration of his friends (tho they would not accept his kind legacies) and the prevention of any mifchief befalling the company from his dying in their hands. It is probable, if he had finifhed his will, he would have added other legacies; for feveral Englifh gentlemen were kind to him, as well as Mr. Thornton.

The night after Naimbanna had made his will, the veffel, tho clofe on the African coaft, durft not attempt to land, as the wind was contrary, and there was danger of running on the Scarries bank. The next morning how-

however, tho the wind was still contrary, Mr. Graham went off to the settlement in an open boat, to procure medical aid. But when the physician came on board, the poor youth was only just alive: and in that state he was carried to the settlement the next morning, July the 17th, when the ship came to an anchor.

On the first account of Naimbanna's illness, an express had been sent to inform his friends at Robanna: and soon after he landed, his mother, brothers, sister, and other relations came to the settlement. His wives it is probable, lived in some distant part, as they are not mentioned. The distracted looks of his mother, and the wildness of his sister's grief affected every one. His cousin Henry, an ingenuous youth, who stood among them, attracted the attention of all by the solemn sorrow of his countenance, which seemed to discover a heart full of tenderness and woe. His brother Bartholomew was the only one, who appeared little concerned, and gave much offence to the gentlemen of the factory, by the indifference of his behaviour.

In the mean time, the dying youth appeared every moment drawing nearer the close of life. His voice failing more and more, the little he said, was with difficulty understood. Once, or twice, those around him caught hold of something like our Saviour's words, *Many are called, but few are chosen.*

About an hour before he died, his voice wholly failed. He was awhile restless and uneasy; till turning his head on his pillow, he found an easier posture, and lay perfectly quiet. About seven o'clock in the evening of the same day, on which he was brought

brought on shore, he expired without a groan.

When his mother and other relations found his breath was gone, their shrieks, and agonizing cries were distressing beyond measure. Instantly, in a kind of frantic madness, they snatched up his body, hurried it into a canoe, and went off with it to Robanna.

Some of the gentlemen of the factory immediately followed in boats with a coffin. When the corpse was laid decently into it, Mr. Horne, the clergyman, read the funeral service over it, amidst a number of people; and

and finished with an extempore prayer. The ceremony was conducted with so much solemnity, and performed in so affecting a manner, that the impression was communicated through the whole ignorant croud. They drew closer and closer, as Mr. Horne continued to speak; and tho they understood not a syllable of what he said, they listened to him with great attention; and bore witness, with every mark of sorrow, to the powers of sympathy.—After the ceremony was over, the gentlemen of the factory retired to their boats, leaving the corpse, as his friends desired, to be buried after the manner of the country.—We mix our grief with theirs; and shut up in the inscrutable counsels of God, all inquiries into the reasons why so invaluable life was permitted to be cut off, just at the time of its greatest probable utility.

In his pocket-book were found, after his death, two litle notes, which shew the wonderful sensibility of his mind in religious matters. They relate to a cirumstance already taken notice of—the disgust he took at the behaviour of the ship's company.
The

The first seems to have been written soon after he embarked.

I shall take care of this company which I now fallen into, for they swears good deal, and talks all manner of wickedness, and filthy. All these things can I be able to resist this temptation? No, I cannot, but the Lord will deliver me.

The other memorandum was probably written after he had complained to the captain.

June 28, 1793.—I have this day declared, that if Sierra Leone's vessels should be like to Naimbanna, or have a company like her, I will never think of coming.

coming to England again, tho I have friends there as dear to me as the last words my father spoke, when he gave up the ghost.

It was not however without reason, that Naimbanna, who knew his countrymen, had been so solicitous in his will, to settle the state of his health, when he left England. Tho the people appeared pleased at first with the attention, which the company had shewn to their young prince; yet a rumour soon began to spread, and gain credit among them, that he had been poisoned by the captain of the ship;

ship; and a spirit was rising in the country, in some degree fomented, it was supposed, by Naimbanna's brother Bartholomew, which seemed to forebode disagreeable consequences. The company had occasion for all their address to satisfy the people, and bring them to a right understanding of the case; which however they at length with great prudence effected.

THE END.

THE CONCLUSION.

FROM THE WHOLE.

THE obfervations which feem naturally to arife from thefe feveral little hiftories, are thefe.

The two firft exemplify—that if a man of fortune would live moft at his eafe, he muft live *within* his income— that a moderate and temperate ufe of the bleffings, which God hath intrufted to him, affords as much happinefs,

as

as thofe bleffings can produce—much more than a licentious abufe of them ———that his enjoyments are in fact multiplied by diftributing from his overplus to thofe in need—that this can only be done by economy, and the abridgment of many of his own defires—that a religious life is the only means of procuring him *real happinefs in this world*—that fortune alone can never be a fource of happinefs—that no fortune can fecure a man againft the mifery, and diftrefs, which folly and extravagance occafion —that when vice is added to folly, and extravagance, they never fail to pro-

produce in conjunction, a very complicated scene of misery—that a profligate man of fortune is a curse to his neighbourhood: in return for the blessings which God hath given him, he first corrupts his own family; and then by his licentious manners spreads vice, and dissipation through the country—and lastly, that altho few men attain so *perfect a character;* or can be so *basely depraved*, as the two persons here represented—yet in the same proportion, in which they approach the one character, or the other, they will feel the happiness, or misery,

misery, which naturally belongs to each.

In the next memoir, the effects of religion on our *future interests* are chiefly considered. It would be an unfaithful picture, unless it pointed out the temporal calamities also consequent on vice; but its primary intention is to illustrate *the triumph of religion over wickedness.*

The most *accomplished libertine* cannot pretend to more shining qualities, or greater powers of mind, than Lord Rochester possessed. If a man of his parts and knowledge therefore could

could not satisfy himself with his deistical arguments, it is hardly to be supposed, that other infidels of inferior parts can hit upon arguments that are more satisfactory. They should learn therefore to be a little more modest; and to doubt, whether their own conclusions are quite so safe, as they are willing to believe them.

Again, the most *abandoned libertine* cannot enjoy more of the guilty pleasures of life than Lord Rochester did. If then these guilty pleasures, when enjoyed in the highest degree, ended in the keenest distress—if nothing could remove this distress, but a sincere repentance

pentance, and the hopes of forgiveness through the atonement of Christ—if religion thus gave peace and happiness to one of the greatest sinners that ever lived—if it, and it alone could quiet his dying moments, and make him happier in the thoughts of leaving the world, than he had ever been in possessing it—it follows, that the pleasures of sin are merely the baits of wickedness—that religion alone affords solid comfort; and is indeed that alone, on which we can depend for happiness in every circumstance, and in every period of our lives.

The

The last of these memoirs shews religion in that *genuine purity*, in which we seldom see it. Amidst the refinements of learning, and philosophy—the courtesies of the world—the maxims of trade—and corrupting amusements of life—we see christianity tricked out in a variety of dresses, in which it is always disguised, and often deformed. Were we with honest and open hearts, to see religion stripped of all these false colours, it would strike *us*, as it did the *early ages*, to whom it was first preached, with its powerful influence *in improving the nature of man.*

To

To illuſtrate this truth is the buſineſs of the little narrative before us. A rude African comes amongſt us, totally void of all ideas of religion. He is kept aloof from the pleaſureable, and corrupting ſcenes of life. Chriſtianity in its genuine form is placed before him. From his own wants, and imperfections he infers its neceſſity. From its holineſs he infers its truth. He imbibes its genius. He changes his ſavage manners. He becomes a new man. He is ſhocked at vice in the profeſſors of chriſtianity; and ſees no difference himſelf between

between *knowing* his duty, and *practifing* it.

In fhort, the ftory of Naimbanna, is a beautiful illuftration of our bleffed Saviour's injunction to *receive the gofpel as little children:* and it fhould convince us, that if *we are* defirous to receive it in this manner, we fhould endeavour carefully to feparate it from the cuftoms and practices of the world; which is one of the moft neceffary, and at the fame time one of the fevereft duties of a ftate of trial.

FINIS.